Tusitala

Songs of
A
Sailor

Daniel Orr

Dedicated:

"To all those people whose lives have crossed with mine and gave me the greatest journey I could have hoped for."

Author's Note: The watercolor paintings are something new in my life. I was 40 before I ever picked up a paint brush, which only goes to show you never know what you are capable of until you try.

Copy Editor: Lizzie Marsh, Raleigh NC
marshediting@gmail.com

"A work of art which did not begin with emotion is not art" – Paul Cezanne

"There are always flowers for those who want to see them." – Henri Matisse

"Art is about emotion; if art needs to be explained it is no longer art." – Pierre-Auguste Renoir

"There is a battle that goes on between men and women. Many call it love." – Edvard Munch

"Rather fail with honor than succeed by fraud." – Sophocles

"I must go down to the seas again, for the call of the running tide. Is a wild call and a clear call that may not be denied;" – John Masefield

"The two enemies of the people are criminals and government, so let us tie the second down with the chains of the Constitution so the second will not become the legalized version of the first." – Thomas Jefferson

Table of Contents

Big Blue Ball

Sailor Songs

Humor & Fun

Sappy Love Poems

Lyrics I Wrote Down

Second Time Around

Joy, Happiness, Freedom

Chapter 1 – Big Blue Ball

These poems were inspired by watching people or observing the beauty that comes from nature. Often as I drive down lonely highways late at night, my eyes look at all the boxes along the side of the road and realize that inside each one is a family that is as different and unique as falling snowflakes. Each contains different styles, different composition, different ambitions, and each has its own burdens to bear. They probably worry too much and don't appreciate what they do have.

Nature seems so much more organized in its diversity. Every living thing determined to survive in the simplest of ways. Other animals do not judge one another for their actions, yet they respect and protect their place in the hierarchy of all living things: friend, enemy, neutral or food.

Our planet, a big blue ball, rolls over the dark fabric of an endless void, and where yesterday there was nothing today it is filled with an infinite amount of emotions, dreams, hopes, and fears. As the big blue ball spins along its path, that same space tomorrow will be empty and a void again. Nothing of consequence will have changed it, for all the worries and all the triumphs will have passed, and in the greater sense of the Universe our moment was trifling and frivolous.

Once we understand that we are on a personal journey filled with moments, we can learn to appreciate each one. That it is the moments that will define our life. So, concentrate on the present to guide your future. That for the things we can change there is no need to worry and for the things that we cannot change, well, there is still no need to worry. So whether life seems like it's going uphill or down, remove worry from your life and use that energy to observe and appreciate the gift from our maker that is the journey of our lives.

Simply, appreciate what you have. Choose to be happy then happiness will be yours.

Reverence

Have you ever heard a butterfly
soar gently on a breeze
or the hundred step tippy toe
of a caterpillar amongst the leaves?

Have you ever seen a locust hum
rigid notes pounding in waves
or the chewing grind of termites
in a forest's hollowed graves?

Have you ever felt the robin's color
brilliant against the light blue sky
or gray-green spectacle of a brook stone
as swirling waters tumbled it by?

Have you ever known a flower's bloom
the graceful smile leaning towards the sun
or the gentle dew streaming down
collecting, growing one by one?

Have you ever thought to breathe a sigh
and appreciate an eagle's wings
or to promise hope or offer love
to have a reverence for all things?

Kewalo Basin

July fifteenth
    seven in the morning.
I'm already late
    need to get going.
Don't have to work
    friend coming soon.
Drive to the airport
    howl at the moon.
Traffic so tight
    lights won't change!
It has been months
    is she still the same?
Where to go?
    What to do?
What does she want?
    If only I knew.
Beer and brownies,
    breakfast divine.
Nothing planned
    except a good time.
Watching the dolphins
    play like children.
Walking the beach
    brings infatuation.
Gather with friends
    at the ol' factory.
Spaghetti and memories
    all quite satisfactory.
Night time falling
    time to fly away.
Remember my love .... until next someday.

Simple Cycle

country children
playing in a field
leaping hiding
simple pleasures
a butterfly
beautiful flutter
the chase begins
trampled dandelions
fallen ferns
flying out of reach
disappointment
a grasshopper
curiosities rebirth

Morning Sun

I begin each day
with the thought of you.
You are my Morning Sun,
illuminating my world,
filling me
with the warmth of your glow,
reminding me
that each day is filled
with beauty and possibilities.

Homer Alone

The sun has risen over Elysium
The mermaids frolic in the sea
Centaurs and satyrs dance freely
With music and songs just for me
Zephyr feeds us fresh warm air
Dryads join in with their song

In my world of dreams
of fun and sweet memories
I would discover you among the trees
We would walk in this land
where love runs free
I would hold you so close to me

We would escape into a clearing
past Judge Mino's hearing
Where sprites would prepare dinner
just for you and me
ambrosia and apple wine
from Athena's garden divine
watching as unicorns dance by the sea

Apollo's chariot flies from here
The time has come that I have feared
I won't watch you go
I can't make you stay
Teardrops to Poseidon
Are my gifts this day

In my world of dreams
of fun and sweet memories
I walk alone among the trees
here where you walked with me
where love once ran free
where I held you so close to me

Traveler

Traveling across the world,
Many a folk I see.
Yet, people everywhere
Seem all the same to me.

Their voices are different.
Their clothing is too.
But their actions are persistent,
Really nothing new.

They call themselves,
By different names.
They eat different foods.
They play different games.
But their emotions are persistent,
Really nothing new.

So why do we quibble?
Why do we fight?
How can we believe,
We are more right?
Their desires are persistent,
Really nothing new.

Affinity

Take some time to ponder
All the mysteries of the world
Then it's easy to realize
How wonderful simple things are
Like the whisper of waves
Or the blooming flowers
Romance at its finest
Is often not far
Strangers are only strangers
Until they take time to greet
People are closest to nature
Watching the sun set into the sea

Philosophy

Knowledge is the only treasure
a thief could never steal.
Life has no rehearsals
you must do what you will.
Dreams are nice to have,
but goals must be set.
Work for what you want.
Don't just take what you can get.
It's okay to be ambitious.
It's okay to be proud.
Remember we are only human,
don't look down on the crowd.
The finer things in life
are usually the simple ones.
Money is not happiness
but it helps to have some.
For an average man,
an average man like me,
the best that I hope for
is to find the best in me.

Reflected Gaze

Mirrored image of beautiful splendor
Exotic eyes enticing surrender
Light brown hair flows with the breeze
Intricate form designed to tease
Sex appeal exudes through her innocence
Sincere whispers through empathic
indifference
Appealing to all she sees

Everyone Needs Someone

When questions arise
Does life open doors?
Love, knowledge, prosperity?
Come inside the light
To make your choice.
Us and Them are We.

Some will choose love,
their days will shine bright.
I will follow knowledge.
Hoping you will take my way
To become better men.
Some will choose prosperity
which can only lead to greed.
Their days will slip away.
Never ask for too much.
Reward comes all in time.
I look to tomorrow
Hoping tomorrow will come.
I'll be ready when it does.
Never waiting too long
To take life by the reins.
There is a gift in everyone
Wife, daughter, son, father.
Because everyone needs someone
I look for you in the light.
Wanting to discover the love in your heart
And come to be the light in your eyes.

1984

Capitalism, communism
Who has got the better way?
Population explosion, inflation growing
What can the leaders do or say?
People sinning. Where's John Lennon?
Why do people treat each other this way?
Missiles flying, people crying
Stripping all their hopes away.
Who can save them?
How they praise him!
Hoping for another day!
Thirty minutes, no more pennants.
All is lost during the bright display.
Winds are screaming, people dying
Nothing left to do but pray.

<u>Life Cycle</u>

Birth
Innocence - Purity
Wants – Desires - Needs
Knowledge - Appraisal - Judgment
Lusts – Loves - Futility
Wisdom - Hope
Death

<u>Snowy Day</u>

Freshly fallen snow paints the world white
Virgin splendor reflects the suns bright light

Undisturbed blanket covers complete
Until innocence disturbed with children's feet

Hustle and bustle with no where to go
They frolic and disturb the new fallen snow

Snowballs go flying so high and so fast
Hit Daddy quick while the opportunity lasts

Fall back in the powder and gaze at the sky
Waving arms and legs to intense to deny

Forming snow angels there where we lie
Memories of our youth we do amplify

Pushing snowballs over unbroken ground
Making them larger, oh, making them round

Stacking them high one on top of another
Making a snowman that looks like no other

I Never

I never knew the answers
To all of life's questions
I never reaped the pleasures
Of a springtime presentation

I never knew the answers
To the riddle of a love
I'm not sure who God is
Except someone from above

I never knew the answers
To a farmer's simple plight
I never saw the promise
In a sailor's monotonous life

I never knew the answers
To make decisions like a king
Towards the unbalanced scale
Of life and love and things

Day After

The warmth of the sun on my neck compliments the cool breeze washing over me.

This morning, offering new beginnings after narrowly escaping the twisted metal, noise and suffering of yesterday. While the coffers are empty now and the carriage is gone, hope lingers on.

Criminals and government have left my world empty and barren, my love abused and far away.

Though this morn I have the sun, the wind, and the day. Freedom because there is nothing left to lose. No expectations to achieve.

It is wonderful to imagine what comes next.

Chapter 2 - Sailor Songs

From 1985 to 1991 I served my country in the United States Navy. It was an experience that would alter my world view and my personal beliefs. The military is not for everyone but if you are lost and searching and willing to let others tell you how to think, then this might very well be a good place to start adulthood.

I was never very good at following people who couldn't answer the simple question of "why?" and the military wants you to do on command not ask. They preach efficient communication but they practice blind obedience. I was not cut out for the hive mentality.

But the Navy provided transport to some wonderful places on this Big Blue Ball of ours. The world is mapped and has lines drawn on pieces of paper, but in reality there are no lines. We belong to the Earth, we do not own any part of her and yet we're responsible for all of her. She is our life giver.

Whenever people ask me where I am from, I tell them I live here but I am from Earth. It was once held against me in a court of law.

ARS-39

There once was a boy who
went to sea
Lo and behold this boy was
me
I traveled aboard a boat
made of steel
The adventures were few
the dangers were real
We unmoored the
CONSERVER and now she
is free
Set sail from Pearl Harbor
into a glistening sea
Days were exhausting and
nights plain turmoil
Our water was salty the sea
shimmered with oil
Mornings sun rose over a
vibrant sea
Giving life a meaning, a
purpose to be
On the fantail we gathered
to smoke and tell stories
Of Australian women and
English lorries
To visit exotic places was
everyone's dream
Those nights in Samoa we
made quite a scene
Not drunken sailors just
boisterous and loud
We danced in the streets we
sang to the crowds
When the fun was over
it was time to set sail
The CONSERVER was old
and the sea gave us hell

The water rose high and
tickled the bow
The ship lunged forward we
held on somehow
Hours of fighting from being
beaten alive
Some were worried - I knew
we'd survive
Then the moon peeked out
from behind a dark cloud
All sighed with relief then the
silence was loud
Cramped and close quarters
tensions so high
Arguments came easy it
was hard to get by
The skipper came forth and
to us he said
"You're good sailors my
men. Now it's home that we
head."
Spirits arose and friends
were remade
One hundred eager sailors
ready to be paid
A lot of preparation came in
those weeks
With thoughts of our ladies
or beer on the beach
When in Pearl Harbor we
had finally come home
We all disembarked and left
CONSERVER –
Alone

Tides Ebb

A moment of splendor as the Sun
Sets over a restless sea.
The songs of birds succumbs to
The whisper of waves.
The sun is gone but her blood
Still colors the horizon.
The moon majestically takes his place
In the center of the sky.
Stars are his court as they watch
The Earth in silent splendor,
Counting how many sailors perished
To an unforgiving sea.
Grieving stars and their King,
The Lupine Lord.

Secret Admirer

Hello beautiful lady,
Features so unique.
If searching for a goddess' splendor,
It'd be you I'd have to seek.

Recently our paths have crossed,
Yet we have never met.
I'd love to hold you in my arms,
Although you, I would never get.

If another is holding you,
I feel confident there is,
Tell him he is lucky,
If you are truly his.

Please don't think this note obscene,
For that is surely wrong.
No need to worry about who I am,
For soon I shall be gone.

Adorned with your smile,
Enamored by your grace,
Which makes this world,
A more beautiful place.

With all the strangers you meet,
You make ordinary, a celebration.
Taking time and such care,
Your patience with appreciation.

So with my love and admiration,
Enjoy my thanks and these flowers.
For in your selfless presence,
I cherished all the hours.

Sister

Little sister,
What have you done?
School is important,
Life can be fun.
If home is not happy
Then follow the son.
Life is too hard,
When you are so young.
I know I'm not near,
What should I have done?
Your brother loves you.
I'm your father's son.
I cry for you at night,
But what has that won.
Don't give in little sis,
Things can be undone.
I still love you,
You are my one.

Saturdays

Lying alone on a crowded beach,
So much beauty so far out of reach.
The clothes they wear are very slim,
Just me, my towel and a bottle of Jim.
The water is cold, the waves high,
Beautiful bodies swim ever close by.
With all this distraction, I think of you,
Where are you now? I wish I knew.
New Orleans is too far from Waikiki,
I'd give anything, everything
To have you here with me

Shipmates

Feel the wind in your hair,
Salt in your nose,
The CONSERVER steams on
over ocean throes.

Up on deck
Where the Bosun's hang,
I lost an electrician
Named Christopher Lang.
Two hundred fourteen feet long
Forty four feet wide,
How is it, Richard Day,
Can find so many places to hide?

Down in main control
A clinometer swinging to and fro,
New York laughter and lies, watching
Carruthers polishing with brasso.

Thompson has one eye brown,
And the other blue.
Where he is now,
I wish I knew?

Night Watch

Two in the morning,
Warm Hawaiian breeze,
The air is still and quiet,
Man's mind is at ease.
Electric stars are bright,
Shining along the pier.
Silent people passing,
Reminiscing of the years.
A small copper tube,
Not bound too tight,
Sheds empty tears
Throughout the night.
The ships are silent
Absent mechanical sound.
Ghostly sentinels,
No one around.
The stars are hiding.
As is the Lupine Lord.
Reflections in the waves,
Sway as if bored.
Two thirty in the morning,
And nothing's changed.

Sailor's Goodbye

Time and distance have pulled us further apart.
Yet you still hold a space reserved in my heart.

I still remember those brisk spring days,
When you were the flower I adored and raved.

So sincere and kind, so full of life,
I hoped someday you would become my wife.

Time has taught me that will never be.
You're looking for more than what is inside of me.

I still hope before you are gone,
That we can share one more night in song.

I'm sailing away in this coming week,
I'm coming home first, it's you I seek.

I need to feel your touch and look in your eyes,
One last memory to covet before the tide.

I'm on my way home, please be there for me,
The truth of it is, I still love you, you see.

Holiday Blues

It was late one Thanksgiving.
Far from home I was feeling blue.
My mind started wandering,
Into visions that were of you.
I could not help but to think,
How much I still do care.
Imagining the miles between,
Me here and you there.
So I thought I would call you,
Just to see if you were home.
Then I thought it best that I shouldn't,
Because you may not be alone.
Like a morning daisy opening I remember,
When you were here with me.
Spring days, so young, so long ago,
Well before I went to sea.
Reminiscing the glow of your face,
Which always made me smile,
My heart wept from a love
That started as a child.
My hands are numb and wet.
My lips are cold and dry.
My dreams have been sifted away.
My eyes only want to cry.

I groped in the dark for the phone.
I had to call anyway.
To wake you from your somber sleep,
Just to hear you say.
"Thank you for calling me,
That was very kind of you.
But it's late, I have to get up early.
I have things I have to do."
We said our goodbyes.
Gently, slowly I hung up the phone.
We would go on with our lives,
Sailor on an empty pier, alone.

Tragedy At Home, RS 50

Noise thumping in my ears.
My eyes tired of sight.
Where are they now?
Bodies lie in ocean's depths.
Carelessness, disobedience?
Who is there?
Life no SAFEGUARD.
Turn to, turn to.

Chapter 3 – Humor & Fun

What would life be without silliness and playfulness? Here are some musings that envelop the constant fulfillment of mirth in my everyday life.

Friends are the family you choose. I have a very large family and I love them all. They make me laugh but none make me laugh more than the blood relations I created: four smart, sarcastic, wonderful daughters that infuse me with pride.

Find cause to laugh every day, it is food for your soul.

Cherry On The Top

I want you in my kitchen,
Cooking up some trouble.
I want you in my bathroom,
Playing in the bubbles.
I want to have my ice cream,
With the cherry on the top.
I want to lick the sweetness,
I never want to stop.

I want you on the back porch,
In a hot tub built for two.
Come play with my tiki torch,
You know what I want to do.
I want to have my ice cream,
With the cherry on the top.
I want to lick the sweetness,
I never want to stop.

Murphy's law

Ten till ten
On a hot windy Sunday
Working 17 hours
Wasn't a fun day
Six more hours till bed
It's the morning I dread
It only goes to figure, that
Tomorrow is Monday

Death of a Mosquito

****CLAP****
Fall from the sky
Flying Ninja defeated.
Time now to die!
Down on the table,
Writhing in pain,
Do as your able, but
Never to stalk again.
Look at you struggle
Trying to gain your composure.
Don't you know now, your
Blood-sucking days are over.
Sad little mosquito,
Your reign of terror has ended.
Not even PETA, at your death
Is offended.
Laugh hardy - but wait!
Oh no, it took flight!
Damn this monologue!
The mosquito returned to the night.

Peter Principle

Join the Army
play in the mud.
Train to kill the enemy
spill all their blood.

Join the Navy
the world you will see
Eighty percent is ocean
it all looks the same to me

Join the Air Force
learn to fly high.
Don't expect good pay
just expect to get by.

The Marines are still looking
for a few good men.
It seems at last count
they only had ten.

Win a Few, Lose a Few

On this hill I stand alone
And gaze up to the sky.
Black velvet night, Bone white moon
Scintillating stars up high.

I contemplate my place down here
Where my steps might take me.
I ponder of what my obstacles are
And those who might forsake me.

I remember in past occurrences
Things I should have done.
I'm haunted by the visions
Of things I could have won.

Smiling, I remember a promise
Which still I hear repeated.
It could provide some solace
For when you feel mistreated.

So I cry out to the heavens
With all my tormented heart,
Dear Lord please tell me,
When does "win a few" start.

Double Standard

"Don't look at me!" I heard her cry,
Her face down in her hands.
"I'm such a (w)itch! I know you hate me."
"I completely understand."
But I shook my head to tell her "No."
She would have to do better than that.
She said, "It's all these hormones raging
"That makes me want to spat.
"I can't help what these hormones do.
"How they make me ill and cry.
"Some days I feel so bad inside,
"All I want to do is die."
I opened my arms and took her in
A heavy hug I did give.
"You can not die," I replied
"Without you, I would not want to live.
"There is something I'd like to say.
"Since we are on the subject dear,
"Uncontrollable are your hormones
"This you won't want to hear.
"A giant pool of testosterone
"Deep inside of me does dwell.
"That is just another hormone.
"So why do you give ME such hell?
"Remember that little waitress?
"You smacked me and called me a swine!
"I couldn't help but laugh at your hormones
"You can't control yours but expect me to
control mine."

Scruffy the Squirrel

Scruffy the squirrel
lived in an oak.
Across from the castle
and over the moat.
Now all the King's horses
and all the King's men,
Kept their eye on ol' Scruffy
even though he's a friend.
See in this time, of
magic swords and stuff,
Scruffy came to earth
dressed real tough:
bandanna on his head,
and Nikes on his feet,
with a .38 gun
and a bullet in his teeth.
Scruffy was the baddest
squirrel in town.
His name was known
for miles around.
The squirrel that sent
Arthur's men running.
Never to return,
to go squirrel hunting.
So now at the feast when
knights and ladies are amuck,
The main course they serve
is now roast duck.

Patience

"Take me across the river" I said.
But the crocodile did not lift its head.

"Why does he look at me so?" I think.
But the crocodile does not blink.

"Are you toying with me? That's not cool!"
But the crocodile sinks down into the pool.

"Wait don't leave," nearer I go.
But the crocodile no interest does show.

"Take me across the river" I pleaded.
But the crocodile would not give what I needed.

"I'll wait till your ready" then I sat down.
The crocodile's patience was as long as his frown.

"So you won't help me!" I declared in a shout.
But the crocodile would not come out.

"Bye then ol' croc." I turned then to leave.
He leaped out and ate me. I couldn't believe!

Royal Family

I'm Demented
I'm Demented

I'm a crazy kid you see
I'm proud to be a member of the Royal Family
My father is Napoleon, he sits upon his throne
Me I don't know who I am
It's great to be alone

My boarding room is rubber
No paintings on the walls
Joan of Arc lives next to me
Hitler's down the hall
History fills this place
It permeates the air
Caesar plays chess with me
Delilah cuts my hair

I'm Afflicted
I'm Afflicted
I'm a crazy kid you see
I'm proud to be a member of the Royal Family
My mother's Cleopatra, she sits upon her throne
Me I don't know who I am
It's great to be a clone

Author's Note: This started with a song twisting words from a Hymn. My best friend in high school, Thomas Buchannan, began the idea. Beth Meekins replaced a line to make it better. It won second prize in S.I.P.A. 1985

Chapter 4 – Sappy Love Poems

The loves of my life have been many. From a brown-eyed girl I dared to love too much to four daughters whom I could never love enough. When someone enters your life you never know what type of impression they will leave upon you.

Sometimes the feelings are of admiration and other times infatuation, but nothing strikes so deep in the heart as that person who shares and communicates their dreams and expectations.

When they trust you with their most intimate secrets and leave themselves vulnerable, trusting that you will not take advantage of their openness. These moments are sometimes hard to recognize and can happen with a stranger as much as a dear friend. When you take the time to listen, you can discover so much about a person. Living vicariously through them you can expand your own horizons to bounds never imagined.

When someone enters your heart, they stretch it and make it grow. It becomes more resilient and will never shrink again. People claim that a heart can be broken. I believe that it only gets torn and the bigger the heart the easier it is to mend.

Grains of Sand

A trillion billion grains of sand
Exist through time for all eternity
Stretching endlessly both North and South
Washing away into a boundless sea
Azure sky filled with Zephyr's breath
His gentle breeze washes over me
Yet there is no measure of my love
And the wondrous joy you bring to me

(July 2011)

<u>*Across My Heart*</u>

I etched your name into the sand,
the evening tide washed it away.
I dreamed your name behind my eyes,
the morning stole it away.
I drew your name across the sky,
the wind swept it away.
I signed your name across my heart,
there will it forever stay.

Promise

I love you so deeply
I love you so much
I love the sound of your voice
The way that we touch
I love your warm smile
Your kind thoughtful way
The joy that you bring
To my life every day
I love you today
As I have from the start
And I'll love you forever
With all of my heart

(February 2012)

Time Taints a Memory

When do dreams and memories
Combine to become fantasy?
Morphing what was true
So it is no longer a reality.
Will night follow day, without
your pure memories within me?

I dream because I do not know what else to do.

Have I dreamed so long
to have you back
That as time draws near
reality will lack.
With years of yearning
how I've imagined you'd be.
Maybe I'm wrong in thinking
that you even want me.
There are questions I ask,
answers I'll never know.
Yet everyday I hope
but only time will show.

Power

Lean easily against the back of my neck
Rapture from olfactory senses
Touch of an angel into tired muscles
Ecstasy as my body tenses
Perched above out of sight
Not too low - not too high
Kneading flesh wanting more
Subtle glimpse of peripheral thigh
Virgin time has unsullied sight
Experience a score apart
In this moment time stands still
Blood rushes through my heart
Such ambitious desire
To attract femininity favor
Her future so bright
Seems an unfortuitous labor
Venerable man's dream
Rise up his hoary head
Holding her in such esteem
Her presence my bread

I Waited

I waited for you in the cold dark rain.
You didn't call. You never came.
I wondered why you made me cry.
No promises. No lies.

Maybe I just dream too much,
The gentle way that we once touched.
I can't escape these deep desires
In my soul you are a fire.

I waited for you in the cold dark rain.
You never called. You never came.

Crystal Eyes

I cannot hide when I look inside
Those beautiful eyes, those beautiful eyes.
I swim in them with deep desire
That sparkle, that fire
inside those beautiful eyes.

Forgive me if my tongue is dumb.
I'm not sure where you came from.
It seems I got lucky some how
To find you here with me now.
Those eyes make me succumb

Lost in a dream - trapped by your gaze
Those beautiful eyes simply amaze
No telling how lovely you are
I can't see past those sparkling stars
I can't remember more joyful days

On the Outside

I drive too fast
I go too far
I drink too much
At this old bar
I can't help myself
I just like what I see
I know the youth
Inside of me
And on the outside
I know I'm getting old
But on the inside
I am still just as bold
I retain the spirit
Of a twenty-year-old man
I can still hang in there
For as long as you can
Before you count me out
Consider that the skills
Have been practiced for so long
They're sure to give a thrill
And on the outside
I'm not as pretty as I was
But on the Inside
I am just a boy in love

Meld

When last I heard you whisper,
My heart filled with joy.
The world seemed so far away,
Just a girl and a boy.
Two souls together
Set the Universe apart.
Silence was our blanket.
We had but one heart.
Entwined flesh so tight,
Merging to become one:
Our heat, our fire,
Brilliant as the sun.
When last I heard you whisper,
I knew that you were mine.
The world seemed so far away
Lost in another time.

Exotic

Her face a glow, warming hearts
A smile so bright fires start.
Dark tresses falling, silky sheen
Jealous is Esmeralda, the Gypsy Queen.
"¿Cómo estás?" she wants to know.
Fantastic places she wants to go.
"Follow me to Rome!" I tease.
"Let's go to Venice, if you please."
A dream, oh a dream, I want to believe.
Her voice is a song but the words do deceive.
Still there is no other who shines as she does.
Despite her grand gifts, insecure is her love.
Imagine softness like cumulus clouds.
Spirit so bold, but not tainted or proud.
She carries herself with confidence.
Beautiful and devoid of arrogance.
Her attire does fit her exotic style.
Her laughter, pure, does beguile.
She makes my heart beat fierce like a puma
I say to her, "Quiero ser tu pluma"

Daddy's Doubts

Little one's learning so fast and so quick.
How can I teach you all life's little tricks?
How do I explain very simply to you,
Why the sky chose its color to be blue.
What do I say when you ask, "What is rain?"
Why do clouds float and why don't the trains?
Is grass always green? Are trees always tall?
Why are cats and dogs different and mice so small?
Daddy, don't you know that girl down the street?
Her daddy has hair on his face and his feet!
Is there something wrong and you don't want to say?
"No," I reply, "some people are just that way."
What can I do to try and explain it all?
How do I soften my little girls fall.
When she realizes there is no magic here.
How will I help her overcome all of her fears.
How will I know if she's fully prepared?
How do I show her I will always care.

Breakfast

She looked at him as if to say
But then she never did.
Turned her gaze into the bay
And there her thoughts she hid.

He looked down to the butter in the pan
Simmering softly, melting slow
How she felt in that moment
His heart might never know

So across the room he softly crept
Eyes fixed upon her thighs
In his hands, her face, he took
To look into her eyes

Gently lift the crows did fly
Her smile so full, aware
Gazing down he kissed her crown
He knew that she still cared

She tucked her face against his side
He held her soft but strong
Pushed his fingers through her hair
Blonde, beautiful, long.

In the loud silence
Two souls became one
All the world faded away
Until everything else was gone

Two Rhythms, two hearts
Gently did converge
Flesh pressed so tight
Emotions begin to surge

Close his eyes, her scent so sweet
His nose against her hair
Finger tips trace her shoulders
So happy that she's there

No words between them needed
Presence was their passion
She was tan and he was pale
Together all the fashion

Without a smile her face did rise
And when her eyes met his
To one knee he did fall
Conquered as her wish

Fingers nimble through his hair
She scratched him like he loved
Placed his face between her breasts
He wore her like a glove

Protector and Savior, lover and slave
She was his passion, life to his breath
Confident, redeemer, lover and slave
He was her passion, gave her life depth

Gentle kiss upon her breast
She pulled him closer against her
Tightly did he take her waist
Both hearts begin to stir.

Lifting her as he stands, Around
His neck her arms do fold
Lovingly, Silently takes full control
She loves that he's so bold

Across the bay the breeze so strong
The scent of the sea in the wind
Sunlight shines into an empty room
Where love was reborn, again.

Chapter 5 – Lyrics I Wrote Down

I am not very musically inclined, but I do like to sing much to the chagrin of my children. I play a little saxophone and less piano. I do not have the patience to figure out the guitar.

But I like to sing to myself and sometimes Something comes out that has potential.
But the words are an expression of whatever I was feeling, from sad to silly, lonely to in love. Maybe one of you will find the chords that fit the stanzas and send them to me.

What do you call such a body of work? Oeuvre - The sum of the lifework of an artist, writer, or composer?

Nah, too French. How about simply: Lyrics I wrote down.

Paradise

I wake up each morning
With a warm breeze in my hair
And the smell of the ocean
Means I don't have a care
I just spent all night
Dreaming of you
With a flower in your hair
And all the things that you do
I realize it's paradise
With you in my life
One of these days
I'm gonna make you my wife

'I realize it's paradise
With you in my heart
One of these days
We'll make a great start'
(repeat)
Paradise
Warm breeze in my hair
Paradise
No, I don't have a care
Except for you

You Still Drive Me Crazy

Sometimes at night I think of you
I don't know what else I can do
'Cause baby – you still drive me crazy
And sometimes I still cry
No matter how hard I try
To forget how much you gave me
I can walk into a crowded bar
But I still wonder where you are
'Cause baby – you still drive me crazy
I know someone else is holding you
I know you told me we were through
But baby – you still drive me crazy
I know I am a fool to wait for you
But there's nothing left for me to do
'Cause baby – you still drive me crazy
I wonder about the life we could have had
Sometimes it drives me completely mad
And baby – you still drive me crazy
You still drive me crazy.
(spoken)
I wanna thank you
For the time you gave me
Even if it drives me crazy
(sung)
And Baby, you still drive me crazy

When I Look at You

She was dancing in her own world
Standing there this beautiful girl
Her eyes sparkled like a dream
My world seemed so serene
I had to take a few steps closer
To find out who she was
I think she was an angel
I don't why it's just because
(Chorus)
It's when I look at you
I can see heaven in your eyes
It's about time you knew
These feelings I can't disguise
There is hope that fills my heart
Even though we are worlds apart
It's when I look at you,
That I know you're the one for me
I see the crowd but they don't see me
Wondering what your dreams could be
I stand and watch you sway
Listening to the music play
I want to know your name
Hold your hand and walk in the rain
Wake up just to see your smile
And know you were here all the while
(Chorus Repeat)

Little Bird

I remember how I
met you
On a dock by the sea
Our dreams we
shared
said you were for me
You're a Little Bird
so wild and so free
Just a Little Bird
You mean the world
to me
As the sun set down
Over an azure sea
The world faded
away
there was only you
and me
Entwined fingers in
your hand
I showed you my
passionate heart
You picked me up
then set me apart
You're a Little Bird
so wild and so free
Just a Little Bird
You mean the world
to me

We lay right down
I held you close to
me
All the stars came
out
You were all I could
see
You're a Little Bird
so wild and so free
Just a Little Bird
You mean the world
to me
That day has gone
Just a fond memory
Do you recognize
How your heart
saved me
With an open heart
A spirit so pure
You were the
medicine
You are my cure
You're a Little Bird
so wild and so free
Just a Little Bird
You mean the world
to me

Trio

Well I love you, and I love you too
You make me as happy as I can be
I love the way that we just kiss
It's as simple as it can be
When we're together late at night
And it's just we three
I like the way she kisses you
While you're kissing me
I love the way that we do touch
The feeling just sets me free
And the way you play with her hair
When she is loving me
Now both of you are just twenty-two
Allow your love to set you free
So rest your head upon her chest
Just feel that chemistry
Well I love you, and I love you too
I can't believe this has happened to me
But I promise to love my best
Just like when I was twenty-three
The way she feels against my skin
Fills me with energy
The way she looks against your skin
That just amazes me
Well I love you, and I love you too
There's not much more I can say
The two of you know what to do
To really make my day
I can't believe how much I love
Loving you two, loving me
It makes me feel just like a man
Like nothing I could foresee
Well I love you, and I love you too
It's as simple as it can be
I'm the luckiest man there is
My god, I'm glad I'm me

Dared To Love To Deeply

She had raven hair and sparkling eyes
The kind of beauty you cannot hide
Creative, artistic, dreamer, and fun
I knew this girl would be - be the one
But we were young and did not know
Just, which way our lives would go
I wanted her there was no doubt
But not all our dreams …. work out
And I dared to love too deeply
I dared to love so long
I dared to love completely
Just to find out that I was wrong
(guitar)
Sometimes I think about her
And wonder what her life brings
Does she know that I think about her
Does she know that she's still in my dreams
But we were young and did not know
just which way our lives would go
I wanted her there was no doubt
But not all our dreams work out
And I dared to love too deeply
I dared to love so long
I dared to love completely
Just to find out that I was wrong
(Guitar)
We were young and did not know
Just which way our lives would go
I wanted her there was no doubt
But not all our dreams work out
And I dared to love too deeply
I dared to love so long
I dared to love completely
Just to find out that I was wrong

Why Must I Wait For You

Why must I wait for you
What do you have to do
Just say that we are through
Or say you love me too

I wait beside the phone
I'm tired of being alone
I wish that you'd come home
Tell me how do I atone

Why must I wait for you
What do you have to do
Just say that we are through
Or say you love me too

(Instrumental melody)
I know that I was wrong
That's why I wrote this song
Why can't we get along
These nights, they are so long

Why must I wait for you
What do you have to do
Just say that we are through
Or say you love me too
(Instrumental Melody)

If You Wanna Do It

Don't you order me
another glass of wine
I know what you are
scheming
I can tell by the way you look
at me
I know just what you're
thinking
And I look in your eyes
I see you just realize
This is the chance you've
been waiting for
So, just pay our bar tab
then let's go an' catch a cab
let's find out what's in store
So if you wanna do it
Let's get down to it
Cause I wanna do it with you
And if you won't say it
Don't know how I'm gonna
play it
But I know I'll play it with
you
So if you wanna do it
Then let's get down to it
We can do it together
And if you wanna do it
Cause you know I wanna do it
It's not like it's forever
I can see your hands are
shaking
But don't you think I'm faking
Yes, I'm nervous a bit
But if you wanna do it
Then let's get down to it
I won't stop till you beg me to
quit

So if you wanna do it
Then let's get down to it
Cause I wanna do it with you
And if you won't say it
Don't know how I'm gonna
play it
But I know I'll play it with
you
So if you wanna do it
Then let's get down to it
We can do it together
And if you wanna do it
Cause you know I wanna do it
We could pretend that it is
forever.
We don't know where its
gonna take us
But we know its gonna shake
us
And make us happy for a
while
So if you wanna do it
Then let's get down to it
And let me make you smile.
Now if you wanna do it
Let's get down to it
Cause I wanna do it with you
And if you won't say it
Don't know how I'm gonna
play it
But I know I'll play it with
you
So if you wanna do it
Then let's get down to it
We can do it together
And if you wanna do it
Cause you know I wanna do it
We could do it forever

Third Cup of Coffee

I'm on my third cup of coffee
Looking at the clock on the radio
It's telling me that I'm late again
As if I don't already know
When I woke up this morning
You weren't there lying next to me
I tried to convince myself, that
I don't care but that's a lie you see

I'm on my third cup of coffee
Staring at the clock on the radio
I'm already late for work
I really just don't wanna go
Now I am thinking it's too late for me
To even make a show

I'm on my third cup of coffee
Ignoring that clock on the radio
They'll do without me just as well
That old job and boss can go to hell
I worked there for twenty years
They don't deserve my tears
Like you, they never appreciated me
So now I'm free

I've finished my third cup of coffee
I'm tired of looking at the clock on the radio
I'm going back to my bed
Maybe I'll see you in an hour or so

Come Back to Me

If you loved me then
Why did you go away
If you love me now
Why don't you come to stay
I don't know what happened then
You never said why you left that day
Come back to me please
I'll make it okay (x3)
You are my dreams
My ecstasy
You're in my heart
We were meant to be
I love you so
Please hold me
Come back to me please
We'll make it you'll see (x3)
Can't you tell
The feeling is right
I'll need you tomorrow
I need you tonight
I'll tell you I love you
And hold you so tight
So stay with me please
We'll make it all right
We'll make it tonight

<u>Come On Over</u>

You like movies
Well, so do I
You like the girly ones
That make us cry
You like sushi bars
I want Chinese food
You tell me your stories
I like listening to you
So why don't you come on over
Spend some time with me
I can rub your shoulders
You can tell me about your dreams
Don't worry babe it's ok
If it's only for a little while
I don't mind if you can't stay
I just want see your smile
We can watch some movies
I'll try not to cry
Order some take-out food
I want you babe, that's no lie
So why don't you come on over
Spend some time with me
I can rub your shoulders
You can tell me about your dreams
Don't worry babe it's ok
If it's only for a little while
I don't mind if you can't stay
I'm gonna love you anyway

(Nov 2010)

You Can't Help Who Your Heart Likes

Well I went out with her
But I was thinking of you
I guess that means
We may not be through

I know you said good-bye
But my heart still longs for you
Can't make myself believe
There's nothing left to do

And you can't help
Who your heart likes
You can't help
Who lights up your life
She may not be your lover
She may not be your wife
But you just can't help
Who your heart likes

Chapter 6 – Second Time Around

I never planned on starting over at forty. I guess I had it too easy and the gods wanted to see if I had the resolve to do it all over again.

I've been fighting Meniere's Disease and spending a lot of time on my back watching the world spin and wondering what it might all mean. One thing I have noticed is that when I fall down, everyone around me panics. I inform them that there is nothing to be done but wait. But still they fret, try to find me comfort and worry. I just lie perfectly still and watch the world spin. It doesn't hurt physically.

It is frustrating for someone that has been so in charge of their life. It is an entirely new dynamic. No one wants to hire a man that falls down without warning. Everyone wants to express their sympathies but no one wants to help you help yourself.

I smiled when I realized it was the same old thing. When I was young they would say they wanted someone with experience and I would ask, "How do I get experience if no one will give me a chance?" Now that I have experience, they want younger people they can train and invest in.

The world is a fickle place. If you can find a little niche to fit in sink in your nails and fight to stay there. Now that I have tons of free time I have discovered that it is wonderful but comes with a curse. Without the funds to entertain yourself, all this free time is as confining as any cell or worse - navy bunk. But writing is free, so here are few of the 60+ poems that have made it to paper. Thanks so much for reading my book. It took me a lifetime to fill.

Why Do I Go?

"Why do I go?" she asked one night.
"I like to talk, if that's alright?"
"Surely, there's a better place."
"There might be." I said, as I cupped her face.
She looked deep in my eyes and just waited.
I leaned in close and kissed her, unabated.
She blinked not once but twice then said
"How did I let you get into my head?"
"Your head is not my goal, but it's a start.
"I have aimed deeper to find your heart."
"I didn't give you my permission," she objected.
I closed my eyes and then reflected.
Her face was still cupped inside my grasp.
So I kissed her again like it was our last.
She laid her head upon my shoulder.
She was young and I much older.
She closed her eyes and fell asleep.
I enjoyed the moment as I weep'ed.
She was light yet my body was aching.
Quietly I felt my older heart breaking.
Because I knew, it would not endure.
She was my relief but not my cure.

Cuddling

Two bodies relax and melt into one another
A father and his child, or perhaps two lovers
An affinity there, a bond indestructible
So quiet and soft and most unremarkable
The worries of the world all fade away
As we hold one another and gently sway
Two heartbeats, two minds, one loving embrace
Gently, securely, now watching your face
The sound of your breath, the smell of your skin
The warmth of your touch, all is akin
To the simple necessity that we all desire
The acceptance of our faults - entire
The forgiveness and expressive love
The adoration offered pure as a dove
Simple and spontaneous, no plans to muddle
There is no feeling better than to cuddle

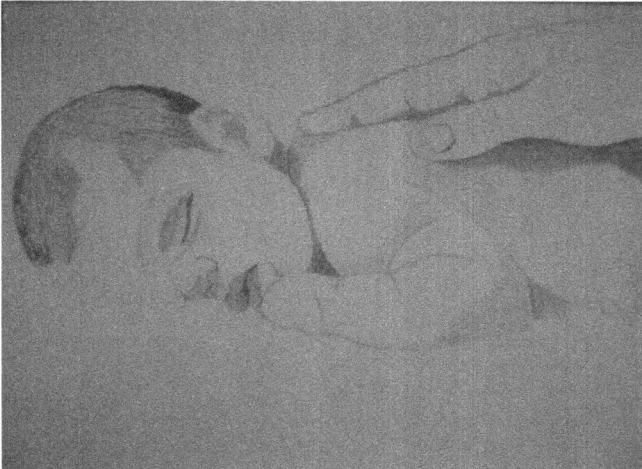

Midlife

Shattered hopes
Slighted dreams
Hopeless wishes
Foolish games
Truthful lies
Mobile waiting
Watching skies
Children playing
Adults running
Closed-minded
Clouds raining

<u>Stalling</u>

Even though you're not here,
Some love has lasted through these years.
Once lost and alone without you,
Every precious memory still holds true.
Cold nights go slow, hot days are forever,
Another dream lost,
of when we were together.

Escape with me once again,
sincere touch of life.
After a long forever,
forgotten from my sight.
I have carried the memories in my heart,
You're part of me,
intertwined to tightly to part.

My Harlequin

When the sun rises for a brand new day,
Before my eyes open I can see your face.

I know I'm half dreaming as I think of you,
But the smile on my face is stuck like glue.
The warmth of the sun against my skin,
Makes me feel like a kid again.
The warmth you create against my heart,
Empowers me for a brand new start.
I don't dream about ships or oceans blue.
Italian wines and fancy foods won't do.
Money talks but it can't sing like you.
How do you do it? I have no clue.
Scintillating stars are all so bright,
When I think of you in my arms at night.
And they shine in heaven for me,
But your face is all I can see.
So the sun moves through the sky,
The night hides all the reasons why.
And all the love that I feel inside,
Is a feeling I can no longer hide.
You are a song played by a violin
If I were religious, you would be my hymn
For you I'd go out on a limb
Just a dream, my harlequin

No More Tears

Once I listened to a song on the radio,
About a girl I didn't even know.
The words were soft and sweet and slow,
I could not stop them, the tears just flowed.
Once I watched a T.V. show,
About a boy I didn't even know.
His life was lost. He didn't know which way to go,
I could not stop them, the tears just flowed.
Sometimes I sit in the morning sun,
Sometimes I have the urge to run.
Sometimes I wonder where is the fun,
And the tears would fall, one by one.
Then to my life, you came in,
You became more than just a friend.
It's a feeling I don't want to ever end,
I know the warmth that your heart sends.
Now the tears no longer flow,
The dreams I have just grow and grow.
This is a love I have never known,
All my tears have flown.

Arms

As my eyes wash over you
I feel the hunger
Desperate gaze, descending view
I feed the hunger
As my mouth presses against
your lips
I feel the gentle lift from your hips
Soft and sweet and delicate
A precious treasure
I purr so hard to make you wet
A sensual pleasure
I know the hunger you realize
When with a shudder open thighs
Swollen flower all in pink
Opens to my view
Longing tongue in pink does sink
So thus the passion grew
Hard is the rise from down below
Ready and firm with no place to
go
Smell the sweet scent of her
innocence
Melting for my mouth
Splay her flesh with confidence
Tongue slips through then out
Hold her tight to keep her still
Listen to her body as it bodes her
will
Arms stretch out and nails dig in
I feel the sweet stings
Against my scalp she rakes my
skin
Fingers are her wings
Fleshy button so hard become
As I lash her with my tongue
Feel the way the earth does move
Beneath this silken 'scape
Nuzzle through her woman's
groove
Erotic pleasures over take
How her body dances to and fro
As I explore her so very slow

My heart beats fierce within my
chest
As my body begins to rise
Tonight she will know no rest
When I gaze into her eyes
Left then right my lips do tease
Folding her form with rising knees
Between her my face does pause
Soft gifts so full and free
Circling kisses paint the globes
Which she is offering me
Lick the tip and make it moist
Exhale a hot deep breath by
choice
Watch the brown so tight become
When delicate and slow
I tease her round with my tongue
Hear her breath gently blow
Then feel the way her body eases
How I give to her and how it
pleases
Rest her feet on shoulders high
I move to move against her
Press my hips against her thighs
Her throat begins to purr
Feel the flesh not moist but wet
Soft center opens as she gets
Enter slow, no regard for time
Descend to depths unknown
Press my lips against her mouth
And catch her softly groan
Flesh does dance between our
lips
Flesh does move between our
hips
Two as one, I find such bliss
Pleasure, I have never known
Her embrace and impassioned
kiss
Desire, to make her my own
Caught in the web of her charms
Regretless, I surrender, to Arms

Tailored

Though it leaves me naked, I should confess,
I would not have you remove your dress.
For in your natural state of splendor,
Lustful desires could I only render.

Masseuse

At your mercy, under your hands,
Strong muscles wane as wants demand.
My strength fades in your touch so tender.
My mind drifts, feeble, as I surrender.
My heart drums on like a parade, tragic.
I cannot see them, those hands of magic.
Ten sorceress' wands casting a spell.
Emotions so primitive does she impel.
A dream, just a dream, her touch sincere,
What fortune of fate has brought her here.
Through panting breath, I cannot escape,
These selfish longings that she creates.
This feeling of bliss should never abate.
The feeling of one who gives, appreciates.
Her hands, two vixens, do tease and explore.
Forever I beg, forever I implore.
She laughs at me, emasculated.
She leaves my heart, invigorated.

Different Feathers

A songbird was bright yellow.
Her song attracted an older fellow.
Owl perched high in the sycamore tree,
Listened to the songbird with much glee.
In the sun, the songbird flittered about,
Inside the tree and sometimes out.
She always came back to sit and sing.
The owl would peek over his wing.
Sometimes when the darkness shrouds,
The owl would soar above the clouds.
While the moon shined very bright,
He felt her song throughout the night.
Softly, would he land beside her nest,
Listening to her heart beat inside her chest.
Slightest of grey, just before dawn,
With a deep sigh, the owl would move on.
To perch among the highest branches,
Wisdom he held, yet pondered his chances.
No sadness could fill his heart,
When at dawn her song would start.
Her music to him did please,
And place his mind at ease.
Tucking his head inside his wing,
He dreams as she does sing.
His mind succumbs to slumber,
And in his dreams, above the lumber,
They would soar over ground.
She was yellow and he was brown.

Her tiny heart beat fierce and true,
His keen eyes could not undo.
The difference between their two worlds,
Not so simple as just boy and girl.
Many years had he seen before she came along.
Many years had he lived before he heard her song.
In her song, life and love abounded.
In his wisdom, did he sit confounded.
Day became night as night became day.
Weeks became months, could he go on this way?
Waiting and listening,
Watching and hoping,
Thoes yellow feathers bright,
Could brown feathers might?
The owl took a chance, asked if he could stay.
The songbird without a sound, simply flew away.
The oak tree is green.
The night quiet, serene.
The owl does not fly,
Only the tree knows why.

Phoenix

Labyrinth removed
The world has stopped spinning
Doubled is my sight
As I start my new beginning
Like a child
I begin to learn to walk
With each step I take
Into my future I do not balk
Today I laughed when I realized
My life was purged by flame
Flesh burned from my hand
And started my life over again
With new wisdom and fewer ties
Time to begin to live again
Free from the anchors that held me down
I will dance, dance in the rain
One step at a time
A new journey begins
Open these wings
Ride on these winds

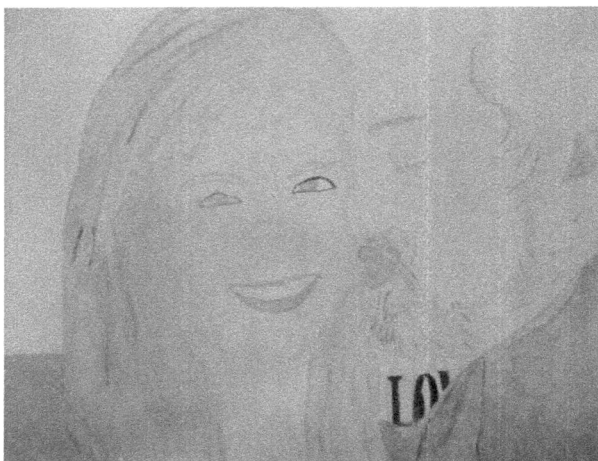

Chapter 7 – Joy, Happiness, Freedom

Is she beautiful? Yes, inside and out. But that was not what drew me to her. She was fragile and irregular enough that she frightened people, so she was misunderstood. I was not afraid. I wanted to understand. That is what drew me to her. For all of her feminine wiles and intimate desires, these were but drops in an ocean of why I came to love her.

Even when she left suddenly, abruptly, it was not because she didn't love me or I her, but instead was the flight response to her fears of abandonment. I was not trying to push her away. I was trying to get her the help she begged me to find for her.

Her self-mutilations drove her to greater depression and although the cure existed, she could not recognize it nor could I provide it to her on my own. Evil took away her pain by taking away her mind, but they only wanted her body.

She is still beautiful. And I am still not afraid. Now, I do understand. And it is what pains me to let her go but there is no greater hopelessness than trying to cross an ocean alone. "Water, water, everywhere and not a drop to drink."

I fear she has drowned in her sorrow and can no longer be saved, but I will love her always.

The Journey

I found you frozen in time,
Deep and dire without hope,
Shared with you all that was mine,
Mostly, just gave you my time.

I had not loved but did not know
Until a love did inside me grow
An unprepared circumstance
Taught my soul and heart to dance
Together we journeyed near and far
With love so bright, the brightest star
Apart from all the others
We two became such lovers
Oh, what tide upon us came
Held your hand throughout the rain

Then medicine man did poison give,
Until your mind could no longer live,
From the edge you fell so fast so far,
The light burned out, my falling star.

"Please help, please help, I am not right"
Your darkness shrouded out the light.
"Should I get lost, will you save me?
I think I might be going crazy."

Bad men fed your fears and strife,
I lost the girl who was to be my wife.
Her mind so clouded she forgets,
I love her still, my heart does fret.
Poison, poison, a living death.

Tonight these tears I shed for thee,
Tomorrow you shall shed for me.
For all the pain my heart begets,
Tomorrow will be your own regrets.

For good but wrong they poisoned you
And stole away a love so true
Clouded thoughts you could not see
Although not perfect, perfect for me

If only your mind could be free of blight,
Reminiscing the truth and love so bright.

While laws and judges do not agree,
I did all I could do, please forgive me.
So today, again, I find you gone,
"Rotting with your rights on."

Tonight these tears I shed for thee,
Tomorrow is so hard to see.
For all the pain my heart begets,
Tomorrow will be your own regrets.

Allow your Heart to Sing

As I look warmly upon you today,
I wonder what words could convey.
Truth about what tomorrow could bring,
If only you would allow your heart to sing.

For here there are no riches to wear,
No gold nor diamond tiara for your hair.
Absent are the servants many,
Bills and debt are a gracious plenty.

But here inside these simple walls,
True love whispers, true love calls.
A simple gesture of flowers I bring,
If only you would allow your heart to sing.

Pearls and lockets, or emerald bracelet,
Wealth eludes me, I can not fake it.
Dream if you must of jewelry galore,
But life's no game there isn't a score.

Come with me and what you will find,
Is an endless love in this heart of mine.
Fountain of adoration, a wondrous spring,
If only you would allow your heart to sing.

Promises in the dark are made by men,
Who long to commit original sin.
Who only want to feel your affection ,
Without concern for your heart's reflection.

But here in the absence of your touch,
Grows a love still that has grown so much.
Passion for her actions as she does her thing,
If only you would allow your heart to sing.

Paradise plenty is not where I live,
I have no treasures for which to give.
Material things that bring brief pleasure,
I possess too little to bother to measure.

But rest gently in my chair with me,
And find yourself some serenity.
Know that love is a firm security,
That unlocks the soul and sets it free.

Not for a minute, an hour or a day,
Forever is how long I wish you to stay.
You'd be my Queen and I'd be your King,
If only you would allow your heart to sing.

When Her Daddy Died

She was only three years old when her daddy died.
It was such a shock for them, how her family cried.
Selfishly they did what comes so naturally.
They forgot about the child who was only three.

The teenager became mom in that broken home.
Suddenly the three-year-old became so alone.
No one knew what to do when their daddy died.
No one could see the little girl dying inside.

Time would pass the girl would grow to be so beautiful.
All the pain she hides inside no one would know.
She would laugh and she would play, shine so wonderful.
But deep inside the fear and pain, they would steady grow.

She would fail at life, over and again.
All the things she would try, she could never win.
Deep inside she would cry,
On the outside she would lie.

She acted like that child who was only three.
Why don't you care? Why don't you love me?

Suddenly her life just tumbled down.
Pieces of her world lying all around.
With nothing left and hope all gone,
This seemed the end of this girls song,
Then suddenly he came along and took her to his world.

There she would find some time for peace of mind.
She could not share nor trust at this time.
Hidden deep inside, even from herself,
Was the child that died inside when her daddy died.

For a year the two would grow into a family.
Demons she held inside
He would sometimes see
He'd take her hand, hold her heart and smile so gently
Asking her to let it go
That girl that's only three

Time for you to grow up and to understand
What happened was not your fault. Cry if you can
Then realize that each new day
Is a chance to move away
From the pain of the little girl who died inside

Now you are on the run fast as you can
Escaping from love and such a caring man
The truth it hurts, the work is hard,
Nothing will heal those scars
But the pain can go away, yes they can

Accept the help of this loving man
Trust the heart of this loving man

And deep inside, where there resides,
A three year who still cries
Let her out so she can be free.
Let her out so you can be free

Kylie Lynn

Dear Kylie Lynn
    Please let me in
        Your story's not new to me

Give our love
    A chance to win
        Please help me help you see

You are not a prize
    Upon my eyes
        But a song unto my heart

Your silence comes as no surprise
    Thou silence fuels my heart's demise
        Give forgiveness a chance to start

Crazed I ran
    A dire vicissitude
        Dark clouds would hide the days

I have some clue
    Why it came unglued
        What drove your mind away

Each breath you take
        Apart from me
                My heart shall never mend

You're lost my dear
        I can't shake my fear
                Drugs, the tools of evil men

Our love's a wealth untold
        More precious than silver or gold
                I lived dreams inside your eyes

Pleasure burst from your fingertips
        Joy I have tasted upon your lips
                Sweet passions betwixt your thighs

Come again to my heart so pure
        Restore that love which is the cure
                Our family your heart's desire

No dream is lost
        By cold winter's frost
                When love is a raging fire

Sweet Casey Lynn
        Please, let me in
                Give our love a chance to win

Run Away

Running from the dream hurts less than losing it.

Life is scary. New love can be terrifying.
When it has never existed before.

Happy faces laugh and play,
But there is not a single day,
When you are not missed by all.
These walls that were a home are now empty halls.

The girls still ask, as if I could know,
How you are and where did you go.
I tell them I wish for you to be safe,
Hoping you find a happy place.

Our birthmarks match just like our souls,
The dreams we had were matching goals.
I resent my country for what they did,
I do not blame you for why you hid.

Home, hope and love still abound,
Because of the joy that we had found.
None was better friend, wife and lover.
Irreplaceable, there will be no other.

The girls remind me and always say,
They miss you every day.
I say, "Me too, but we must move on."
You were the music to my song.

A final thought and not poetic in the least.

My entire life has had people in it with mental illness. They are not retarded nor bad people. They are different not less.

I have told many people that life is all about choosing. Choose to be happy or choose to be sad. I allowed my children a choice even at young ages, calling them the 'happy way' and the 'sad way.' I offered guidance and opinion but have insisted that the choice was theirs. For the mentally ill, that ability to choose is not there. That is why it is an illness.

Some people will abuse their circumstance and shun responsibility, but for the true mentally ill this is not a choice. They are not retarded. They are different not less. Impulsivity, Mania, Learned Helplessness, Depression, Delusions, Splitting, Disassociation, and other symptoms are as real as a fever or a cough. No one chooses to have an illness. I hope you all can find a place in your hearts and minds to try and understand mental illness and eliminate the stigma, discrimination and apathy surrounding this varying but very real health condition.

Legislators have written into law safeguards to protect our loved ones. But law does not exist in the court rooms of North Carolina.

A faction of elite citizenry has taken over our Judicial Branch of Government. These lawyers have made themselves the only electable citizens for the role of Judge, claiming that knowledge of law is required. But consider that not even the position of President of the United States has an educational condition for office. This is because our elected officials should be chosen for their wisdom and not some varying educational credential. Let lawyers explain to a wise judge and let justice prevail. For now, the courts are a game of skill and cronyism and no justice exists there.

Thank you for reading my poetry book. I hope you found some poems that made you want to re-read them again in the future. Before we part, I wanted to share a classic story that inspires my life daily in helping others.

After a heavy storm a thousand starfish washed ashore. A little girl began throwing them in the water so they wouldn't die.

"Don't bother dear," her mother said, "there are too many. You won't make a difference."

The girl paused for a moment and looked at all the starfish on the beach. Reaching down she lifted one up and showed it to her mother. "It will make a difference to this one." Then she returned it to the sea.

Other titles by me are not romance novels but novels about true romance themed in mental health.

Casey - Don't Ever Call Me Worthless, Jan 2013
A Life Worthwhile, Jan 2014

www.ingramcontent.com/pod-product-compliance
Lightning Source LLC
Chambersburg PA
CBHW071827020426
42331CB00007B/1640